The Secrets of Success

To Whom It May Concern:

Let no one tell you that you cannot achieve your dreams. Reach for the stars! Because at the end of the day, those that spoke negatively against you will one day serve you.

Copyright © 2019 Ronnie House Jr.

All rights reserved

ISBN: 978-1-7903-9143-1

Welcome To My World!

Take time to dissect each page of this book to achieve a better understanding to unlocking your most defined potential and your greatest breakthrough.

– Ronnie M. House Jr.

Table of Contents:

1. The Foundation..5

2. Success Leaves Clues...7

3. A Changed Mind..10

4. The Commitment..12

5. Character..14

6. Integrity..16

7. Write the Vision and Make it Plain....................................17

8. Intentionality..19

9. Repetition..21

10. Confidence...23

11. Maximum Activity in Short Periods of Time............................25

12. It's not an Overnight Gig, but Small Steps Perfected in Quantum Leaps..27

Prayer of Salvation...29
To be Born Again..30

Chapter 1: The Foundation

"Therefore whosoever hearth these sayings of mine, and doeth them, I will liken him unto a wise man, which built his house upon a rock: And the rain descended, and the floods came, and the winds blew, and beat upon that house; and it fell not: for it was founded upon a rock. And every one that hearth these sayings of mine, and doeth them not, shall be likened unto a foolish man, which built his house upon the sand: And the rain descended, and the floods came, and the winds blew, and beat upon that house; and it fell: and great was the fall of it." — Matthew 7:24-27.

Foundation – what does that mean? Well, the Webster's definition explains it fairly well, and that is: a basis (such as a tenet, principle, or axiom) upon which something stands or is supported. Did you get that? A BASIS upon which something STANDS or is SUPPORTED is a foundation. That is insane! But what does that have to do with me? Well I'm glad you asked! It has a lot to do with you. How? "For where your treasure is, there your heart will be also." And in my words, this signifies the strength in which your world is built upon. And in the words of Zig Ziglar, "The foundation stones for a balanced success are honesty, character, integrity, faith, love and loyalty."

So tell me more on what you're trying to illustrate about this foundation theory, House. Sure! The reason why the foundation is the first point I would like to make on my secrets to success is because without it, everything else will crumble. You can be the highest building on the planet, look the best, and have all of the most luxurious items in the whole world, but without a strong foundation, does that really matter? And if you answered yes, then this book is specifically for you. As you continue to read along, this concept of having a foundation and a strong one will make more and more sense to you in the long run. In fact, let us get to that point right now.

What foundation are you talking about? The foundation that I'm implying is neither physical nor tangible, but something that can be seen upon you, something that you carry with you at all times, and something that will represent you even after you are gone. And that is The Kingdom of God! "For what shall it profit a man, if he shall gain the whole world, and lose his own soul?" – Mark 8:36. This is why your foundation is so important. I've seen it too many times not to explain that this is the key to a long, prosperous and successful business and life. This is why T.D. Jakes has so many celebrities wanting to be around him in the likes of Oprah, Tyler Perry and Diddy Combs because they understand that the key to a happy, longevity type and positive environment is the basis on which it is built upon.

      Is your foundation built upon the Word of God? If you don't know Jesus, then I kindly recommend that you get to know him. You may not realize this, but you will need him along this journey we call "life" because I kid you not; life is hard without Jesus, but simplified with him. To know God is to love God, and what better way than to start off your life with him being the Chief Cornerstone. In the back of this book, you will find a Prayer of Salvation that you can repeat after me to accept Jesus as your Lord and Savior. It's the first step, or what I would like to call Destiny step that will propel you into "your" future.

Chapter 2: Success Leaves Clues

"One reason so few of us achieve what we truly want is that we never direct our focus; we never concentrate our power. Most people dabble their way through life, never deciding to master anything in particular."
— Anthony Robbins

    Didn't you know that success leaves clues? Over the most recent years of my life, I took the time out to study millionaires and what I have found out is quite shocking: that is that they are teaching you the game for FREE, but many people are allowing it to pass them by because they are unable to recognize the words in which they speak. Did you catch that? Billionaires and Millionaires are showing you how they made it so you can climb the same rope, yet people get jealous from the things in which their money can buy, but won't take the time out to apply the rules and concepts so that they could have the same. That is what's wrong with this generation – people don't want to learn how you did it – but yell give me the money in the same instance. Whereas, this does not apply to you since you took the time out to buy this book, read it and pass it along.

    These are three reasons as to why people miss out on this opportunity: #1 it's because success recognizes success. Now I want you guys to picture a diamond buried slightly underneath the gravel on a sidewalk in which you walk every day. You can barely see it, but the reflection of light against the sun makes it to stand out in an unusual way. So you walk this path for the past three days paying not too much attention to this reflection of light because you assume that it's just a part of the sun's crepuscular rays, and you just go about your business until one day, you notice that the sun's reflection isn't shinning in that particular spot, but you think nothing of it and go about your day once again. The very next day after you have gotten home, you noticed the TV turned on the news, so you sat down on the couch to listen for a while. There are two people on TV, one in which a lady is covering the story and a guy smiling is explaining his behalf. Suddenly you notice that they're reporting on the sidewalk in which you pass every day, so you turn up the volume and are more focused on what they are saying. The lady asked the man how he discovered this 100 million dollar jewel, and to explain what was going on in his mind as he made this discovery. The man said, "Ma'am, I wasn't even supposed to be on this street. I got chased by some dogs that broke loose from their chains, and I was just trying to avoid them so I came down this street looking for cover, but as I was looking for a place to hide, I saw this weird looking light, so I thought to myself, 'I might as well see what this is about,' and it's like I forgot all about the dogs because this light was so captivating. So I walk up to it and I noticed that it was buried in the gravel underneath, so I started removing the gravel to figure out what this could possibly be, and BAM! There it was a diamond. Ma'am, the only thing going through my mind was that I'll never have to work again." Now how would you feel if you were that person walking by every single day asking God to bless you with what you need, but failing to recognize the blessing right in front of your face? Angry, right? Depressed? Maybe even a little upset, huh? Oh yea, I'll definitely be upset as well, yet this is happening all over the world. Every. Single. Day.

    #2 People only want what you have, but not through learning it themselves. Have you ever heard the saying, "Give a man a fish, and you feed him for a day. Teach a man to fish, and you feed him for a lifetime."? Well, the same rule applies here. People expect handouts in life only to find out that the hustle isn't free, but is sold separately, and when they do, they leave (for whatever reason) never investing in their own lives nor become the example that many have done for them and their family who knew success not.

    #3 People are not willing to grow. Nobody wants the process, but everybody wants the reward. In a recent study, it was shown that 80% of Warren Buffett's day involves reading. Now if one of the wealthiest men in America continues to work on his self-growth, even at his age, why can't we? The answer is standing right in front of us! How many of you guys can honestly say that you work on your personal growth at least twice a week? Once a week? And how many of you guys don't do it at all because you're too busy? Well, that's not an excuse. Because if I had a million dollar check in my hand, and all I needed from you was at least an hour a day for you to work on personal growth, how many of you would find time to make that happen knowing you had a million dollars waiting for you at the end of your journey? Wouldn't we all? But what happened to you being so busy? See, it was never a busy issue because people find time to do what's most important to them, but it was a priority issue. Meaning you lacked to see the value of "personal growth", but is quick to fund another man's dream out there on the football field. But you don't have to be that guy. I'll explain why in the next chapter.

Chapter 3: A Changed Mind

"Progress is impossible without change, and those who cannot change their minds cannot change anything." — George Bernard Shaw

      This is probably, by far, the most controversial topic in this book. Why, you asked? Well because if most of the people in today's society would understand this information, a lot of the issues that we're dealing with as a society would be solved by now. It's just that simple, but not that simple. It's simple because it's an easy concept to apply to your life; it's not that simple because we have to shift and direct our focus intentionally which we as programmed humanoids will have to break out of the box to do. Let me explain.
      So what does it take to acquire a changed mind? Well there are multiple variables used in achieving this success, but we are going to cover the main ones that will help you go from a caterpillar to a butterfly. Aphorism #1 – Who you hang out with on a daily basis will identify the path in which you will walk. In other words, if you show me your circle of friends, I will show you your destination. And this is true for any person whether you're black, white, Hispanic, poor, rich, know Jesus or not, it has no specificality to it. Now I want you to take about 8 minutes and think about who's all in your circle. Okay, good. Now I want you to think about what gifts, talents and abilities you would like to learn or know. Good. Now go find someone of that caliber, who exemplifies excellency in their character and integrity, and who's 10 times better than you are (but we can say about 4 to 8 times to be more realistic), and begin to build a relationship with them. What you will come to find out is that your way of thinking will change. Your actions will rise to the occasion of excellency, and your brain will begin to emit new waves. Before you know it, your patterns and your routines will be in alignment with that of the one greater.
      Aphorism #2 – It takes a couple of days to break a bad habit, but it takes one day to start a new one. To simplify this statement: go out and create new habits daily. Now I understand that this is easier said than done, but if

you don't try, will you ever succeed? The medal is only given to the person who decided to take the first step, this initiative. Do something you've never done before! Go to bed early, pick up a book (hmm), or turn off that TV and CHOOSE to brainstorm on your dreams and goals. The rewards are endless! Wouldn't you agree that it takes doing something different to achieve something different? I mean don't expect to do the same thing over and over and expect different results – it won't happen!

For me, the greatest challenge was first to recognize the problem, then come up with a plan of action. For instance, I had got out of my normal routine of going to bed early, I'm pretty sure you all can relate to this, and I knew where my consequences would lead me (I've been down this road before). So what did I do? Well every day after I messed up my routine (for it took me a couple of days to recognize it), I started chipping away on how long I stayed up and forced myself to go to sleep earlier and earlier. It was quite a painful process because my days felt shorter and shorter, and it was like I'm just wasting time (which I dislike the more than anything). But this forced me to become more productive which made me sleepier as the night time approached which in turn forced me to get up earlier and earlier. And before you know it, I was back on my routine and the habit was wiped away. So if this is you and you're struggling to overcome that bad habit, think about how wonderful your life would be without it then go to work!

Aphorism #3 – Continuing the course even if it's overwhelming. And by this I am simply stating that you must be disciplined following your course of action. To be disciplined is not an easy task because you have to force yourself to be focused on the prize regardless of how treacherous and unbearable the road may be, but I GUARANTEE YOU that it will all pay off in the end. I've never met a person to say that disciplining themselves in certain areas never paid off, so for it to start today it must be ludicrous.

Chapter 4: The Commitment

"I've missed more than 9,000 shots in my career. I've lost almost 300 games. 26 times, I've been trusted to take the game winning shot and missed. I've failed over and over and over again in my life. And that is why I succeed."
— Michael Jordan

Are you committed to the dream? Now I'm pretty sure you answered yes to the question, but who doesn't? Yet we see many people who gave up on their dreams when times get ruff. It is the rough times that make you, break you then build you back up again. I choose this particular quote because Michael Jordan's story is the epitome of what not giving up looks like. We've all witness his greatness through the good days and the bad, yet he was committed to the end to finish what he started. Let's look more into that.

It all started back in 1978 at Laney High School in Wilmington, N. C. There Michael Jordan was a 5'9" sophomore trying out for his high school's varsity team, but little did he know, they would choose the other sophomore over him by the name of Leroy Smith. Leroy was a 6-foot-7 forward in which the coach favored over Jordan because "height" was badly needed. That reminded me of when I tried out for my college team and the coach choose my cousin over me because height was needed as well. You would think that at this time that a kid in that position would accept the facts of not making the team, and would maybe think to themselves, "That's it. I won't make it; I give up." But not this kid — not Mike Jordan — in fact, it did the complete opposite. Bruce Banner let out his emotions, and this is what it came to be. In the words of Mrs. Ruby Smith, Michael's physical education teacher, "He never wanted to lose in anything." And so that fire manifested even more. So more that every single day, Michael Jordan was in the gym before Mrs. Smith got to work — and this was between the times of 7 and 7:30 am. He was so driven from the thought of how he didn't make the team that Mrs. Smith had to run Michael out of the gym, but it was worth it, it was worth it. Fast forward to his junior year, that Mike Jordan that you heard of was a different breed now. No longer was he the 5'9 shy player that his teammates made fun of, but he was an assertive 6'3 guard who couldn't be stopped. He dropped 35 points during his first varsity game. He then went on to average, in two seasons for Laney, 25.4 points, 12 rebounds and 5.3 assists per game, and the rest was history. This is a great illustration of what it looks like to stay committed to the cause, and to never give in.

Chapter 5: Character

"Knowledge will give you power, but character respect." — Bruce Lee

Now we all can spit out the definition of character verbatim, but do we really understand what it means to live this out is the question. For character is the moral or ethical quality that defines a human being; whether you're black, white, Hispanic or Latino, it's all the same. Just like how character plays an important part in placing you within today's society, it also determines the altitude of your success. This is why I chose to talk about this topic as being one of the greatest secrets of success today (and by now, it should be during the first three months of 2019 in which you have picked up this book and begin to read). I've seen it destroy countless celebrities' lives because it didn't at first start at the root, and anything you didn't learn growing up will shine a greater spectrum over your adult lifehood. This is real, and if this is your first time learning or hearing about this, then the time is now. You have the ability to choose — make a good one.

Great character is not something you can acquire overnight. It is something that life will either teach you or train you into being — for it is an endless process of growth, maturity, love and care. A step to acquiring great character is to always be a man or woman of your word. And what I mean by this is to tell the truth 100% of the time. If you say you are going to do something, do it. Don't half do it or not do it halfway. For character is defined by what you say you're going to do, and it takes an even longer time to gain that trust, that you have acquired with someone, if you do not follow through with what you are saying. I've witnessed this for myself as a young musician for my local church. It took me a while to realize that my musical director didn't believe a word I said. It didn't hit me until I asked them for a favor dealing with the support of my business, and their reply, "Why should I believe you? You've lied to me countless times about you practicing for the week, and then when we get here you haven't done anything. So why should I trust you?" That hit me hard. So what did I do? I started analyzing my life (this is something that I do quite often when I am out of alignment with anything I got going on), but I didn't still quite get it. It took me asking for support of my business, when I started to understand things a little more clearly, that the light bulb came on. "I get it!" I said. "That's it!" I replied. "I must show them that I am a trustworthy person on saying what I am going to do!" So I went to work, and not only that, but I saw the lack of motivation that I had, and what was needed to influence or make a difference in my life. So the next couple of weeks following I didn't say I was going to do anything (for they didn't believe me anyways), but I just went to work. "Ronnie." They said. "You practiced for the week?" "Yes, I did." "Okay, show me." Boom. Next week: "Ronnie, you practiced this week?" Yep, I replied. "Okay, show me." Boom. And as weeks and weeks passed by, I was beginning to see a level of great friendship and trust based off of me stepping up to the plate on keeping my word. And from this day on, it has opened up many doors that I could not have imagined if I were still stuck in my old rubbish habits.

Chapter 6: Integrity

"One of the truest tests of integrity is its blunt refusal to be compromised."
— Chinua Achebe

    Integrity, what is it? What does it consist of? These are questions that people oftentimes ask, but the answer is right in front of them. Integrity is defined as the quality or state of being whole or undivided. When I think of this word, I see a man who's consistent in his daily routines of his daily actions. For instance, if he's serious about picking up his trash from eating, he will do just that. No matter the time or place, you can always expect him to be a man of his word.

    This is the key to integrity. Will you change just because others may think it's of little to no concern, or will you be so moved with compassion that you can't help but to lead by example? This is a true characteristic to leadership. No great leader has ever led with little to no integrity; it's all in the pudding. When I think of integrity in the form of a leader, a great story comes to mind. If you haven't already read this book, I would recommend that you do so forthwith. The name of the book is called *Hero of Hacksaw Ridge*, and the leader that comes to mind is Desmond Doss. In this book, Desmond is faced with ridicule, trials and tribulations, sleepless nights, and at the brink of death with every step he takes, nevertheless, his course was never rewired, and he stayed true till the end. He fought endlessly saving hundreds of his battle buddies with his own life. In the book, you'll see that (with him being the medic) it was his job to aid his battles whenever they went down, and in one particular case, it was the enemy on one side, his comrades on another, and one of his battles right in the middle of war, nonetheless, he ran out there in the middle of the valley of death to save his life. Bullets, grenades, mortars were all in the midst, but that didn't matter to Doss because he was a man on a mission, and a man who's on a mission cannot be shut down.

Chapter 7: Write the Vision and Make it Plain

"If you aim at nothing, you will hit it every time." — Zig Ziglar

I cannot tell you how true this statement is! If you pay attention to millionaires and billionaires, I can assure you that they have a vision board that they visit daily. It's so simple, yet people walk past these billion dollar tactics every day. Remember when I said success leaves clues? Well here's another one! If you catch this one, I guarantee you that success will follow or your money back!

This quote by Zig Ziglar is so profound that I don't think too many people quite understand it. It's true for today's time, back in the dinosaur age and the future to come. Sadly, many people have chosen to take this route in life because it's the most secure with no risk at all. You have to take risk if you desire to become successful. Writing this book is a risk in itself. It could not be read by a single soul; I could make no profit and get no publicity from it feeling like I have wasted my time. This is why many people only dream of being successful, yet they have a full-blown confidence in building someone else's. Now I'm not against working because if a man doesn't work, he doesn't eat, but what I'm saying is why work to build someone else's dream yet doubt yours? This is why I choose to write this book! This is why I chose to reveal all that I have learned from millionaires and billionaires! This is why I do what I do because if nobody believes in you, just know that I care!

In a study done by Dr. Gail Matthews, a psychology professor at the Dominican University in California, she tested the art and science of goal setting. There she gathered two hundred and sixty-seven people – both men and women from all over the world – from different walks of life including entrepreneurs, educators, healthcare professionals, artists, lawyers and bankers. She divided the participants into two groups based off of whether they wrote their goals and dreams down or not. She discovered that those who wrote down their dreams and goals on a regular basis achieved their desires at a significantly higher level than those who didn't. She found that you become 42% more likely to achieve your goals and dreams simply by writing them down on a regular basis.

In fact, this is how I got started with my first ever published book. The start date of when I started gathering my thoughts and ideas happened on a beautiful Sunday morning around 5 a.m. To be exact, it was September 9. I was meditating on things I wanted to see come to pass then boom, it hit me! The ideas started flowing, and I was like a madman with a pen. It was so intense that I had to force myself to put down my pen. It was, for sure, one of my greatest moments and memories of 2018.

I'm a living witness that this concept works! Give it a try. Stop what you're doing and write down at least 5 dreams and goals that you want to see come to pass, and tell no one about them. Then take some time out of your day to meditate on your goals and dreams to come up with a plan and a solution to bring them to fruition. You will begin to see your answers fall from the sky onto your paper, notebook or laptop (however you chose to write them down). Do not hesitate to write them down. I've missed out on phenomenal ideas on things that would have been brilliant because I was stuck in dream world. Do not make that same mistake. And watch what will happen to life as you apply these concepts and step outside of your comfort zone to being a better you.

Chapter 8: Intentionality

"That split-second of intent that you have after you hit your alarm off will determine if you ain't waiting for success to come and knock at your door, but to chase it down, letting the whole world know that YOU AIN'T AFRAID TO TRY." — Ronnie House Jr.

What wakes you up every morning? Is it the sweet smell of honeysuckles outside your window, or is it the soothing waves on your bed? Could it be that you just love waking up because of the things you have planned throughout the day, or could it be from the joy your kids bring you when you make them happy and feel special on the inside? Well, whatever your "what" is, it has to be intentional.

To be intentional is quite simple: all you have to do is zone in on what you want to get done and do it. It's just that simple. Now, I know what you are thinking. You're wondering, after you chose to focus on a certain thing, where do I go from here? Well I'm glad you asked. Because after you have focused on a goal and dream, you just do it. For greater details on the steps, focus back on the previous chapter.

Now I'm not saying just do it without having an idea or plan set in stone because that is absolutely absurd, but what I am saying is that you can have all the information you need to get the job done, you can have all the mentors in the world giving you high-quality advice, or even the help from a friend or a love one, but if you're not willing to act on that idea, it won't come to pass. That is why to move with intentionality is such an important key to the continuation of your growth and your success.

I find it so funny that people think reaching the kind of success that Oprah Winfrey has can't be done, but fail to realize that she's no different from everyone else. The only difference is that she chose to take a leap of faith in pursuing her dreams, and as you can see it paid off. She didn't inherent her riches and wealth, nor was she born in to it, but she made up her mind that she was going to differentiate from the rest, and that the world would know it.

Oprah was born in 1954 in Kosciusko, Mississippi, to a teenage mother, but raised by her grandmother. At the age of six, she was sent to live with her mother who worked long hours as a cleaner. When she was nine, she was raped by one of her cousins, and over the next few years she was sexually abused by other men. She went to live with her father in Nashville at age fourteen; hiding the fact she was pregnant and gave birth to a son two months before he was due. He died shortly thereafter.

Could you imagine what was going through her mind with all of this happening before the age of fifteen? I couldn't, but she didn't allow her downfalls to determine the altitude of her success. She could have just given up on life due to her circumstances, but the lion in her (intentionality) wouldn't let that be. This is why she became the first female African American billionaire in the U.S! For further information on Oprah's biography, you can find it online here at www.biography.com/.amp/people/oprahwinfrey-9534419.

Chapter 9: Repetition

"Whatever we plant in our subconscious mind and nourish with repetition and emotion will one day become a reality." — Earl Nightingale

    That quote by Earl Nightingale is so true. If you constantly do it over and over, whether it's within your mind or actuality, it will become your reality. Just like picking up a basketball for the first time. You might be the worst player in the world, but the more and more you pick up that ball, the more and more you fail to dribble it correctly, you will soon master it. I've noticed this in myself when I pick up a sport or activity. I may or may not do horribly well, but the more and more I focus on a particular thing (with me I go all in) I get better and better. This is the power of repetition.
    Now there are always two sides to every coin, and what I mean by that is that just because you do a thing over and over doesn't necessarily mean that you will get better at it. You can't put in no time and energy and expect to receive greater results; it won't work. That is what we call insanity – which is doing the same thing over and over expecting different results. I had to learn this the hard way.
    Back when I stayed in Birmingham, there was this guy by the name of Dirk. He stood just above being 6'2, and we were rivals. Every day we would be in the gym (I think he was, I'm not sure, but for me definitely) going at it to see who was the best. Back in high school, he made the team and I did not. I didn't let that stop me. Even though he had experience over me, I knew that if I worked hard enough (he beat me every time we played 1 on 1 lol) I could win. So I went to work. No help but a ball in my hand, I did what I thought was the best that I could do. I practiced on this and studied on that while analyzing this and studying the greats in basketball – I knew that I couldn't fail, but each and every day was the same. "Umm, yes ma'am. I am ready to order. Can I get an L on Monday; hold the cheesy L on Tuesday, no hard L's on Wednesday with a side of 4 for 4 L's for Thursday through Sunday please!" This frustrated me every time because I put in all of those hours of work, but yet came down to the same predicament. Something had to change.

So after getting beat countless times, I say down and meditated on the error of my ways. That's where it hit me. It was at this very exact moment that I was thinking about insanity, and on how foolish I was to do the same thing expecting different results. So I changed up my game. There I noticed a difference in how the way he played me, I was becoming a threat. And after 200 games of losing (yes, I know that is a lot of L's), it was finally my time, my moment. It just so happened to be on my birthday as well (neither he nor anybody else knew because I kept it a secret). It was at this moment that we came down to a one shot win game. I had the ball, heart beating profusely, but I knew that if I don't win now I would probably never win. Focused, zoned in. My mind was on the hoop and nothing else I could see. Faked left, then right. I could see the finish line, but the final boss was in my way. It's either I take the shot or miss the opportunity due to fatigue. I let the ball go. Floating in mid-air, all I could think was swoosh! I gave it my all on my last shot, the release felt good. Could this be my moment? Find out next time on Drag… Wait. Swoosh was all I heard, victory was mine.

Chapter 10: Confidence

"If you really put a small value upon yourself, rest assured that the world will not raise your price." — Author Unknown

This is a NECESSARY key to achieving your goals and dreams. If you don't have confidence that it's possible in your life, then how can others see what you see? It is true that people can tell if you believe in yourself or not, due to the fact of how convicting it is to you. That is why this is an important factor to being a great leader because your team will move at the pace you give them. If you are determined to succeed and that no one can stop you from achieving it, so will your team be. They won't give in so easily due to the rough times (because we all have them), but they will steer clear of every obstacle and break down the walls which compete with their destiny.

If you feel like you lack in this area, then let me help you to get past you and see that the grass IS greener on the other side. Key #1: Do something you have never done before. This is a great key to becoming more confident in yourself or your ability. This will allow you to see that life was never harder than what we thought it to be. That it was a mental challenge, and not a physical one. We usually lack confidence in ourselves because are so in tune with thinking that it will fail. So what if we fail – at least we tried! And those who step outside of their comfort zone most of the time never come back because they see that it was them who locked themselves in the bathroom, only to realize that they had the key.

Key #2: Put yourself in uncomfortable positions. And what I mean by this is to purposely go or do what you are afraid to do. If you are afraid to speak in front of people, take a public speaking class. If you are afraid of having stickers touch your body (this was me when I was younger), purposely put stickers all around you. If you are afraid of not making the basketball team, try out a 100 times more. Do what you are afraid to do and you'll achieve what other people are afraid to achieve. This is the key to your success.

Key #3: Be who you are called to be. Do not allow others to downgrade your gift just because they can't see the potential in theirs. Oftentimes people will try to bring you down to their level so that you can fit in, but you were never meant to fit in but to stand out! Pay very close attention to those who you call "your" friend. I've seen it happen a dozen of times. Everything will be all jolly until something comes up, then boom! You will see the true them, and never not take it for face value because what a person reveals to you is as real as it gets to their character. Do not be ashamed because you're gifted in this particular area and others are not. Move with great humility, but also never compress your gifting's because of how others will feel. This is where the leadership aspect kicks in because after seeing what you can accomplish, others will follow. Think on a time to where a leader who was not confident in his ways leading a great bunch of people. I can't either. But never forget, confidence is the key that will unlock your hidden potential that even you had no idea of!

Chapter 11: Maximum Activity in Short Periods of Time

"We all have dreams. But in order to make dreams come into reality, it takes an awful lot of determination, dedication, self-discipline, and effort."
— Jesse Owens

Now when you think of this topic, what comes to mind? Does going out and handling things on your own appear first? Well, if this is you, you have a long way to go. And I understand your hustle, I've been there before. Back then I was a one man band playing my own flute, orchestrating my marching band's steps all while directing from the pew. I get it. You feel as though no one has the tenacity that you have, the drive that you have and will hold you back if you guys join forces, but that is exactly what you need.

Now if you were an independent goal setter and doer like me, then that quote by Jesse Owens makes sense, but let's dig a little deeper. "Unity is strength…when there is teamwork and collaboration, wonderful things can be achieved." Did that resonate with you? Did that hit home? No? Well, you still got quite a bit to go. What I'm saying is that you cannot achieve your dreams and goals on your own, and in order to achieve them in an efficient amount of time, you need a team that's all on one accord. Do you get it now? There's not a celebrity today who has achieved all of their greatest feats on their own, somebody was there to help.

Team work makes the dream work. This is what will produce the most activity in short periods of time. Imagine having to compete at a local race in your neighborhood. You could have up to five teammates per event. In this particular event, you chose to run alone. The name of the game was to run ten laps around the park with each member running up to two. You feel pretty confident in your abilities, so you stepped up to the test. You failed miserably. Why? Well for one, the park is exactly one mile in circumference. In another, you forgot to stretch (if this was me, I could have easily won but that's not the point that I'm trying to make). Thirdly, you just didn't have to energy to continue on. So what's the moral of the story? The more teammates I have the quicker I can get out of here. What I just said was something that you should underline, circle or jot down. That statement has more dimensions than pudding pie.

Chapter 12: It's not an Overnight Gig, but Small Steps Perfected in Quantum Leaps

"As your training integrates Mind, Body and Spirit, enjoy the process. Your journey to the marathon finish will last a few hours. Your journey to the start will influence a lifetime." — Gina Greenlee

      Congratulations. You have made it to the last chapter of this book. I hope that I have encouraged you in some kind of way to where you won't just read this information, but will apply it. If this book has touched you in any kind of way, feel free to email me your responses at RhjrSecretsToSuccess@gmail.com. So without further ado, I present unto you Kefȧlaio 12.

      As I was meditating on what I was going to present to you guys, the main thing that was pressing on my heart was to trust the process. Many of you all may feel like all hope is lost, great! That's how you're supposed to feel. Nothing in life was ever achieved without a price. Just think about George Washington Carver or Albert Einstein. Do you think it was a walk in the park for them to achieve astronomical feats that changed today's society? Well of course not, so why should you? It'll make a better story of how you overcame the most trying times in your life. People need something to be encouraged by, something that they can relate to and say, "Wow! If he/she could do it then so can I!" Because if you reached your destination with no struggle at all, was it really worth it? Did you change or impact today's society as a whole? I mean just think about Jesus and on how he chose 12 disciples from all walks of life to change the world. He chose the people that everyone least expected, yet their impact is still going on some 2,000 years later. So if you feel as though all hope is lost, keep pushing because during your trying times that is when you are made. You will come to know yourself a whole lot better. You'll grow in areas that you never knew existed. This is where true leaders are born.

      No matter where you are in life, be thankful and trust the process. Just think about the metamorphosis of a caterpillar. As you can see, it has three stages to life. It's at first bound only to its present state or the ground, then it's stuck in an airborne state to where it gets rid of the old and takes upon the new, then it spread its wings and fly based off of the first dream it once had. I'm pretty sure that the wee bit caterpillar was wondering as to how it would one day reach the stars and enjoy the fruit thereafter, but some never live to see the day because of what could have happened if they chose to believe. Some were too frightful, some got too comfortable in their current state and some just couldn't dream too big enough. You're probably still hearing from those folks today who talk about what they could of became but never stepped out on faith to become. You can change that, but you must first believe in yourself more than anything.

There's a picture going around on the web of these two diamond miners. Go to your internet browser and type in never give up: the two diamond miners. On one hand you have a guy that's depressed because of what feels like there's no hope around. On another hand you have a guy that energetic, locked and focused on achieving his goal. Now what's wrong with this picture? Well, I'm glad you asked. The guy that just gave up was about one or two hits away from achieving his goal, but as you can see, he got discouraged in believing that it all was a waste of his time, so he stopped trying. Isn't it funny how so many people gave up right before they finished the finish line? Well of course it is. From looking outwardly in, it seems as though it would be a simple mistake to stop trying when they were so close, but we don't understand what it took to make it that far. Living the life of an entrepreneur is not glitter and gold at first, but it will soon be thereafter. We know little on what was on the mind of the one who got away. Maybe he was mining for hours, days or even weeks before he felt that way. Maybe he was told that all he had to do was give it all he had and then he would succeed. The world may never know, but what I do know is that those who succeeded have given up plenty times before, but what separates them from those who tried is that they've tried once more.

This is what encouraged me to write this book. Now I'm not saying you won't, but maybe you will understand what it took for me to write this form of literature. It was many cold nights and a lot of terrible days, but TODAY I present unto you to "The Secrets of Success."

Prayer of Salvation
(Repeat after me by saying this out loud)

    Dear gracious heavenly father God, I come to you today as a broken sinner in need of your repairing love. I ask that you heal me, that you change me with your transformative love. I thank you God for caring enough about me to direct me to your most Holy Word, and I accept you into my heart to purify and transform my ways into your ways. I accept you as my Lord and Savior and I repent of my evil and foolish ways. In all these things we ask Jesus that you will shield, guild and protect us as we embark upon this new journey, and that you would remove anything out of our lives that are not like you in Jesus' name we pray, amen.

    Congratulations!! You did it!! You have no accepted Jesus into your heart as your Lord and Savior!! Give yourself a big pat on the back! This is a crucial step to your walk in Christ! But this is not the end, for you're just getting started! Turn over to the next page for the born again experience! Also if you have given your life to God today, feel free to message me your incredible experience at RhjrSecretsToSuccess@gmail.com. I'm looking forward to your responses!

To be Born Again

Now you may be wondering what exactly do I mean to be born again. Well, let us take a look a scripture shall we. To move and walk in your born again experience today requires two things, and the passage of scripture is found in John chapter 3 verse 5. It says, "Jesus answered, Verily, verily, I say unto thee, Except a man be born of water and of the Spirit, he cannot enter into the kingdom of God." It's just that simple. You must be born of the water and the Spirit.

Yes, I would like to be born again, but how? Well turn with me to Acts chapter 2 verse 37 through 38 and let's see what the men and women during the early church times were asking the apostles concerning this very same matter. It reads, "Now when they heard this, they were pricked in their heart, and said unto Peter and to the rest of the apostles, Men and brethren, what shall we do? Then Peter said unto them, Repent, and be baptized every one of you in the name of Jesus Christ for the remission of sins, and ye shall receive the gift of the Holy Ghost." Did you get that? To be born of the water is to be baptized in Jesus' name, and to be born of the Spirit is to receive the gift of the Holy Ghost.

How do I go about doing this? Well, you will need to find a local church (I pray that God directs you to the proper one) and all you would need to do is to inform the pastor, who's over that church, that you would like to be baptized in Jesus name. You would also let them know that you would like to be filled with the Holy Ghost. He or she will direct you from there. If you have taken the necessary steps to become a born again Christian feel free to message me of your empowering times for when either one of these have taken place at RhjrSecretsToSuccess@gmail.com. Thank you again for taking the time out to read my book, and may God bless you to live out these principles in the fullness thereof.

Thank you for choosing to read my book!!

If this book has blessed you in any shape, fashion or form, these are some things that **you can do** to help spread the word for others to pick up this book, and to dig deep and discover their true potential in the business world. You can help by:

1. Hashtagging - #SecretsToSuccess to your Facebook or Twitter posts.

2. Leaving reviews on Amazon for the book – just type in the book title on Amazon to find me!

3. Word of Mouth – telling your friends and family members about how this book has changed your life, and on how it can change theirs!

4. By liking, sharing and following my pages here:
Facebook: https://www.facebook.com/RonnieHouseJr
Twitter: https://twitter.com/RonnieHouseJr

www.ingramcontent.com/pod-product-compliance
Lightning Source LLC
Chambersburg PA
CBHW030555220526
45463CB00007B/3088